Insight Theatre Group
01 - 6271521

There's Always Spring

A comedy

Arthur Lovegrove

GW00381589

Samuel French - London
New York - Toronto - Hollywood

© 1971 BY SAMUEL FRENCH LTD

Rights of Performance by Amateurs are controlled by Samuel French Ltd, 52 Fitzroy Street, London W1P 6JR, and they, or their authorized agents, issue licences to amateurs on payment of a fee. **It is an infringement of the Copyright to give any performance or public reading of the play before the fee has been paid and the licence issued.**

The Royalty Fee indicated below is subject to contract and subject to variation at the sole discretion of Samuel French Ltd.

      Basic fee for each and every
         perfomance by amateurs   Code D
         in the British Isles

The Professional Repertory rights in this play are controlled by Samuel French Ltd.

The Professional Rights, other than Repertory Rights, in this play are controlled by

---

The publication of this play does not imply that it is necessarily available for performance by amateurs or professionals, either in the British Isles or Overseas. Amateurs and professionals considering a production are strongly advised in their own interests to apply to appropriate agents for consent before starting rehearsals or booking a theatre or hall.

ISBN 0 573 02330 1

Please see page iv for further copyright information

CHARACTERS

Brenda

Alan

Mr Withers

Jill

Ian

Miss Watson

The action of the play takes place in a completely empty room of an unoccupied flat in a block overlooking a square in London, on an afternoon in late autumn

Time – the present

COPYRIGHT INFORMATION
(See also page ii)

This play is fully protected under the Copyright Laws of the British Commonwealth of Nations, the United States of America and all countries of the Berne and Universal Copyright Conventions.

All rights, including Stage, Motion Picture, Radio, Television, Public Reading, and Translation into Foreign Languages, are strictly reserved.

No part of this publication may lawfully be reproduced in ANY form or by any means — photocopying, typescript, recording (including video-recording), manuscript, electronic, mechanical, or otherwise — or be transmitted or stored in a retrieval system, without prior permission.

Rights of Performance by Amateurs are controlled by Samuel French Ltd, 52 Fitzroy Street, London W1P 6JR, and they, or their authorized agents, issue licences to amateurs on payment of a fee. **It is an infringement of the Copyright to give any performance or public reading of the play before the fee has been paid and the licence issued.**

Licences are issued subject to the understanding that it shall be made clear in all advertising matter that the audience will witness an amateur performance; that the names of the authors of the plays shall be included on all announcements and on all programmes; and that the integrity of the authors' work will be preserved.

The Royalty Fee is subject to contract and subject to variation at the sole discretion of Samuel French Ltd.

In Theatres or Halls seating Six Hundred or more the fee will be subject to negotiation.

In Territories Overseas the fee quoted in this Acting Edition may not apply. A fee will be quoted on application to our local authorized agent, or if there is no such agent, on application to Samuel French Ltd, London.

VIDEO RECORDING OF AMATEUR PRODUCTIONS

Please note that the copyright laws governing video-recording are extremely complex and that it should not be assumed that any play may be video-recorded for *whatever purpose* without first obtaining the permission of the appropriate agents. The fact that a play is published by Samuel French Ltd does not indicate that video rights are available or that Samuel French Ltd controls such rights.

THERE'S ALWAYS SPRING

A completely empty room of an unoccupied flat in a block overlooking a square in London. A late autumn afternoon

The CURTAIN *rises to reveal a room completely devoid of fittings and furniture. The paper on the walls is rather patterned. A solitary unlit electric light bulb hangs from the ceiling. There is a partly opened door leading to the hall. The room is almost completely dark except for the faint light of the dying day coming from the uncurtained windows. We can see two attractive young people, aged about twenty-five, standing hand in hand, gazing around the room. They are Brenda and Alan. She is dressed in a light summer floral frock, and he is wearing a pair of lightweight trousers and a light summer jacket shirt with a gay coloured scarf as a cravat*

Brenda Doesn't it all look terribly naked.

Alan Bare! I never was keen on that wallpaper, but it looks even more ghastly without the furniture.

Brenda Darling, you said when you put it up that you loved it.

Alan That was when I put it up. I must have been mad.

Brenda Of course, it was the first room you ever papered. (*Giggling*) Remember the first sheet? As you were smoothing down the lower part, the top slowly peeled off and fell all over you.

Alan I wasted nearly a roll before I got the knack of it.

Brenda But after that . . .

Alan I was brilliant. There was no stopping me. (*He points to the electric light switch by the door*) Look at the way it fits around that switch! A professional couldn't have done it better, although I say it with all modesty.

Brenda It's lovely.

Alan The workmanship—yes—the paper—no! It's ghastly. Who chose it?

Brenda You did.

Alan Me?

Brenda We went through the pattern book . . .

Alan I remember now. Your mother was there and she said it would go with the suite she was giving us . . .

Brenda And you said what a good idea.

Alan Did I?

Brenda Yes, you did.

Alan Oh! (*Looking around*) Well, I suppose it's not bad, really. It's because the furniture, curtains and everything aren't here.

Brenda (*moving to the window*) I loved this view looking over the gardens.

Alan (*joining her*) They look a bit bare now. Winter's icy clutch is slowly taking over.

Brenda It makes me sad to see a lovely garden when it's dying.

Alan (*turning her from the window*) Don't look, then. Remember there's always spring.

Brenda I wanted to come back, darling, to see it again. We were so happy here.

Alan (*putting his arms round her*) So very happy, my darling.

Brenda It's a lovely flat, really super!

Alan Then why is it empty?

Brenda I expect the rates have gone up.

Alan Or else old mother Watson in the flat next door puts off prospective tenants.

Brenda She never put us off.

Alan It would have taken more than that old bitch to put us off. We were just married.

Brenda She was rather nice. She really was. You went by her exterior.

Alan That was enough for me. She was a miserable old dragon! Can't stand dragons. I like my women to be beautiful, like you. (*He kisses her*) But you coped. Proper little St George, you were, but you could cope with anyone. You were the only person I ever saw her smile at. She always scowled at me.

Brenda Did you ever try smiling at her?

Alan At that embittered old spinster?

Brenda (*pointedly*) She wasn't, you know! (*She wanders around caressing the walls, then leans against the back one*) It has been nice, coming back.

Voices are heard off. There is the sound of a door opening, and a light goes on in the hall which shines through the partly opened door of the room. Then the door fully opens and the light is switched on in the room, illuminating the solitary bulb. An old man enters, bowler-hatted, dressed in a heavy winter overcoat, with a scarf around his neck. His name is Withers

Withers Do come in, please.
Brenda Visitors.
Alan Prospective tenants. I bet he's from the agents.

Two young people enter, both in their early twenties, Jill and Ian. She is gay and happy, he is spectacled and appears of more sober disposition. They are both dressed for winter, and Jill is carrying an umbrella

Jill (*excitedly*) It's nice to get in from the cold. Oh, I adore this room.
Brenda I like her. She shows taste.
Ian (*looking straight at the "fourth wall"*) I don't like the fireplace.
Alan I don't like him. He doesn't!
Ian And that wallpaper!
Withers A mere detail. You could put in another fireplace and redecorate to your own requirements. This block of flats is admirably situated, only five minutes from the station.
Alan You old liar, it's eight! I remember him now, it's old Withers. He sold us the flat and told me the same tale.
Jill (*running to the window*) Look at the view over those gardens. I bet they look lovely in the summer. Ian darling, do come and look.
Ian (*moving to the window*) Can't see much; it's getting too dark.
Alan Miserable devil, isn't he!
Brenda Well, it is getting dark.
Withers The gardens in the square are kept up in the most beautiful fashion.
Alan Tell him it's an extra ten bob a week from the tenants.
Withers Of course, as tenants you subscribe to their upkeep.
Alan Thank you.
Ian How much?
Withers Ahem! A pound. A week, that is.
Alan (*outraged*) A pound?

Ian (*sharply*) A pound?

Withers Of course, that entitles you to the entire use of the gardens. Very reasonable, considering the joy they bring.

Brenda (*to Ian*) And they do, they're lovely.

Ian Still, a pound a week on top of everything else . . .

Alan (*still outraged*) A pound! That's a hundred per cent increase. What the hell are they growing there now? Rare orchids?

Ian Another fifty-two pounds a year!

Brenda You're right. He is a miserable devil!

Jill But, darling, think how lovely they will look in the summer. All the joys of your own garden . . .

Alan Without having to mow the lawn or do any weeding. That's almost worth the extra quid.

Jill I love this room and the view.

Brenda You wait until you see the rest of the flat.

Ian One room doesn't make a flat, darling.

Brenda Ooooh! I could kick him! (*She aims a kick at Ian's leg*)

Ian neither feels nor notices the kick

Alan Wasted effort, darling.

Withers The rest of the rooms are just as delightful.

Ian What's the kitchen like?

Brenda Now, *she* should ask that.

Jill Oh yes, what's it like?

Withers Admirable. Large, with ample cupboards, waste disposal unit, in fact, everything.

Ian I think the kitchen is most important.

Alan I know his type. He'll have her slaving over a hot stove all day.

Ian You see, we shall be doing a lot of entertaining.

Alan I bet you'll be the life and soul of the party.

Withers Most understandable. Come this way.

Withers turns and goes out of the door

Jill leaves her umbrella leaning against the wall by the window, goes excitedly to Ian and grabs his arm

Jill Come on, darling, I can't wait to see the kitchen.

Jill and Ian exit, following Withers

Alan Well, I don't like him for a start!
Brenda I like her, she's nice.
Alan Do you think they're married?
Brenda Not yet. She's only wearing an engagement ring.
Alan In that case, there's still time for her to opt out.
Brenda She doesn't want to. She's in love.
Alan What, with that? You must be joking.
Brenda Women do fall in love with the most unusual men.
Alan You, of course, being the exception.
Brenda But you might not appeal to her.
Alan Why not? I take umbrage at that.
Brenda You might not be her type. He certainly isn't mine.
Alan I take umbrage no more. Confidentially, she's nice, but
  not my type, either.
Brenda Darling!

They kiss

  I wonder how old Withers is getting on with them.
Alan I bet he's having one hell of a job with laughing boy.
Brenda I know *she'll* like it.
Alan He won't. Look how he quibbled over the pound a week
  for the garden.
Brenda You quibbled over ten bob!
Alan I suppose the cost of living's gone up since then. He's the
  overbearing, pompous type . . .
Brenda Darling, we must be fair. We don't know them. Under-
  neath that pompous exterior . . .
Alan There's a pompous interior.
Brenda We must be fair and not jump to conclusions.
Alan Very well. I will be fair, unbiased, judicious, and completely
  open-minded.
Brenda Good!
Alan But there is one slight difficulty.
Brenda What's that?
Alan I can't stand the sight of him.

Voices are heard off

  Here they come.

Jill, Ian and Withers enter

Jill (*excitedly*) I think it's lovely, really lovely. It's a gorgeous
flat. I adore it.
Alan (*bowing to Jill gracefully*) And I adore you.
Ian I think the bedroom rather small. Very small, in fact.
Alan I knew it! What did I tell you!
Jill It isn't, darling. It will be snug and cosy.

Withers clears his throat rather loudly

Alan That's embarrassed old Withers for a start.
Ian I like a larger bedroom.
Alan Sex maniac!
Jill But those built-in wardrobes and dressing-table are marvel-
lous, and once we got the bed in . . .
Ian But it is small. (*He walks away to the window*)
             ¯ *enda*) What the hell does he want to do in there, stage
a cup final?
Withers As your fiancé said, the built-in wardrobe . . .
Jill I love it. And the kitchen! It's super!
Brenda It is, it is!
Ian I don't live in the kitchen.
Alan I know your type, mate, never washes a tea-cup.
Jill Think what I could cook in a kitchen like that.
Brenda (*to Alan*) *You* weren't exactly mad about washing up.
Ian But the bedroom . . .
Alan But I never complained about the bedroom.
Jill (*in ecstasies*) And the dining-room is lovely, and the bath-
room, lots of cupboard room. I think it's a super, super flat.
Withers Your young lady is obviously very impressed, if I might
say so, sir.
Brenda You may.
Ian I'm afraid I have my reservations.
Alan (*to Brenda*) Believe me, I really am unbiased——
Jill What reservations?
Alan but— I'd willingly punch him one on the hooter!
Ian Just reservations.
Jill (*almost tearfully*) I don't understand you. It's the nicest flat
we've seen.
Ian How many have we seen?

Jill Hundreds!

Ian (*pompously*) Darling, we have seen precisely six.

Brenda He really is a stinker! (*To Jill*) Stand up to him, my dear.

Jill (*determinedly*) Well, *I* like it!

There is a slight pause

Brenda Good for you! Go on! Don't stop now.

Jill (*even more determinedly*) In fact, I've fallen in love with it.

Alan She must be psychic. (*To Brenda*) Tell her she's definitely made up her mind and he can go to blazes.

Brenda Tell him to go to blazes.

Jill Please, darling—please! Why don't you like it?

Brenda Oh dear, back to square one!

Alan I'll try old misery. (*He goes up to Ian and shouts*) Come on! Change your mind!

Ian I still have my reservations.

Alan (*still shouting*) But nevertheless, change your mind, you pompous ass!

Jill What reservations, darling? Surely it isn't the bedroom?

Alan (*still shouting*) You love the bedroom.

Ian Among other things.

Alan (*disgustedly*) I'm flogging a dead horse with him. You try, darling.

Jill What other things?

Ian Well—er, well . . . (*He turns away, then goes and looks out of the window*)

Alan (*to Brenda*) Y'know, we're idiots! What are we bothering about, anyway?

Brenda I like her, and she loves this flat and wants it. We women must stick together. I'll try.

Jill I said—what other things?

Brenda goes up to Ian, puts her arms around him and her cheek against his

Brenda (*seductively*) Do fall in love with the flat, darling, and take it.

Alan (*pulling her away*) You don't have to try that hard.

Brenda Well, he's a hard nut.

Alan Well, let his girl-friend crack him.

Withers May I make so bold as to enquire what your reservations are, sir?

Alan Certainly you may. Come on, misery, let's hear them.

Jill (*coldly*) I'd be more than interested because I love this flat. There's a happy atmosphere about it.

Alan (*to Brenda*) If I didn't love you I'd be mad about her.

Ian Huh! Happy atmosphere.

Jill Yes, it's warm, and happy, and friendly.

Brenda I take that as a great compliment.

Ian Well, *I* don't feel it.

Alan You wouldn't feel a kick up the . . .

Withers It is, as the young lady said, a warm and friendly flat, sir.

Alan (*moving to Ian*) The trouble with you, mate, is you're not warm and friendly.

Jill I feel it's been lived in, really lived in.

Alan You can say that again.

Jill (*suddenly getting angry*) Well, I feel it and you don't.

Ian No, I don't!

Alan He's a creep.

Jill Then there's no sense in arguing.

Withers (*placatingly*) I must say, with all due respect, that I agree with the young lady. I have that feeling, too.

Alan You don't feel anything, Withers, old man, you're just trying to let it for the commission.

Ian (*stiffly*) Forgive my saying so, Mr Withers, but your feelings are not so much atmospheric as pecuniary.

Brenda I must say he put it better than you did, darling.

Jill Ian, that was very rude and totally uncalled for.

Alan Rude, possibly—but the truth, yes.

Ian I'm very sorry, Mr Withers, I do apologize. I shouldn't have said that.

Alan I am reluctant to admit it, but that was rather handsome of him.

Withers That's quite all right, sir.

Alan That's right! You hang on to a possible commission.

Jill It's silly, I know, but I really feel this flat wants us. Us!

Brenda We want you.

Alan Even though it means taking your choice bit of misery as well.

Ian Wants us?

Alan That's what she said.

Ian I've never heard anything so ridiculous! How can a building want you?

Jill Why are you so against it? It's not the rent, we can afford it.

Alan Don't tell us it's the extra quid on the garden!

Ian If you must know, I've got a reason.

Alan Well, spit it out! We're all agog!

Jill I hope it's a good one, because as far as I am concerned it will have to be.

Ian Well—well—you can laugh at me . . .

Alan I doubt whether we shall have hysterics, but have a go.

Ian (*defiantly*) Well, I'm psychic.

There is a moment's silence, then Alan and Brenda roar with laughter. Jill and Withers gaze at Ian in amazement

Jill Psychic? Did you say psychic?

Ian (*even more defiantly*) Yes!

Alan You're about as psychic as a . . .

Brenda Don't be vulgar, darling!

Alan I haven't said anything yet.

Brenda No, but I knew what was coming.

Jill is still staring at Ian

Jill (*suddenly*) Not about this flat. Not *this* flat. Anyhow, this is the first time I've ever heard anything about your being psychic. (*Really angry*) It's just an excuse. You're about as psychic as a——

Alan She thinks the same as me.

Jill —as a—well, it's just a stupid, feeble excuse. Psychic!

Ian Mr Withers, may I ask you a question?

Withers Certainly, sir.

Ian Will you give me an honest answer?

Withers (*with dignity*) I always speak the truth, sir.

Alan What, in the estate business?

Alan and Brenda start laughing

Ian Who were the last occupants of this flat?

Alan's and Brenda's laughter suddenly dies away

Withers The last occupants, sir?

Brenda suddenly grips Alan's hand tightly

Ian That's what I said.

Jill I don't see that that matters.

Withers Why—er—to the best of my knowledge—er—a Mr and Mrs Ashford, or Ashwell, sir.

Ian I thought so. Why did they leave?

Withers Leave, sir?

Jill Ian, what is all this?

Ian Yes! Why did they leave?

Withers I'm not exactly sure, sir. I wasn't here at the time. I was away on sick leave for about six months—a heart attack. When I got back they'd left. But as the young lady said, it's a lovely flat with a happy . . .

Ian Well, I'll tell you. They committed suicide!

Brenda (*frantically*) No! No! No! It was an accident!

Alan (*desperately*) It was my fault! Mine! I was drunk! Pie-eyed!

Jill (*in horror*) Suicide! How did you know?

Ian Charlie Baxter told me.

Alan Baxter!

Jill But he was transferred up North.

Ian He telephoned me this morning at the office. I happened to mention we were flat-hunting and had an appointment to view a flat in Stafford Court. You see, I gave Baxter a lift here on more than one occasion to visit Ashwell. "Basher" Ashwell, he called him. They played in the same cricket team.

Alan He was a bloody awful fielder.

Brenda And he couldn't bat, either.

Jill That's terrible! Awful!

Alan I know, but they still kept him in the team.

Brenda She's referring to us, you idiot!

Alan Oh God, yes! I keep forgetting.

Ian Baxter told me how the Ashwells had been found dead in bed. He thought it must have been a suicide pact.

Alan Trust that clot Baxter to get it all wrong.

Ian He couldn't remember the exact number of their flat, but said if we did happen to be viewing the one they vacated we would soon recognize it by the nauseating yellow wallpaper.

Jill Oh no!

Withers I'm sorry, I don't know the circumstances, sir. I'm sure that you and your young lady would like to talk the matter over alone before you decide. I'll wait downstairs, if you'll excuse me.

Withers exits, leaving the door half open

Ian turns away, moves to the window and looks out, with his back to Jill who stands looking at him

Brenda Oh darling, I feel so helpless, and I do want them to come here.

Alan (*bitterly*) What, even old "death and decay all around I see"?

Brenda Don't, darling, please!

Alan (*contritely*) Sorry, my sweet. (*He puts his arm around her*) I didn't mean that.

Brenda They would be happy here. I know they would. As happy as we were. I know it!

Ian (*still with his back to Jill*) I'm sorry, Jill darling, I really am. I know I'm an old "stick-in-the-mud", but I do love you so much. More than anything else, I want you to be happy— really happy—in our first home. It's so important. (*Almost to himself*) I really do love you so much. (*He turns from the window and faces Jill*) You do understand, don't you?

Alan I'm beginning to change my mind about him.

Brenda He is rather sweet, and he means it. (*Moving to Jill*) Go on, my dear, work on him. Only be quick!

Jill (*suddenly flinging herself in Ian's arms*) Dearest, I love you, too, so much!

Alan Strewth! That *was* quick! Are you sure she isn't psychic?

Jill But if you wouldn't be happy here, I wouldn't, either.

Ian and Jill kiss

Alan (*disgustedly*) Now she's giving way to him.

Brenda I'd have done the same with you.

Alan Never! You'd have argued like hell! Look at that time . . .

Ian I'm not psychic, you know.

Alan You're telling us!

Ian I just made that an excuse. Remembering this block of flats
and what Charlie Baxter told me, I just had to say something.

Alan I never really did like Charlie, ever since he got me run
out when I was nearly on fifty.

Jill But does it make any difference? We are two different people,
darling.

Alan I know I'm different from him.

Ian I know. But it's knowing of the suicide of a young newly-
wed couple as we shall be.

Jill But Charlie only *thought* it was suicide.

Alan (*moving to Ian and shouting*) Oh God, it wasn't suicide, you
stupid clot!

Brenda (*following*) It wasn't, it wasn't. (*To Jill, beseechingly*) It
wasn't suicide, truly it wasn't.

Ian I know I'm a damn fool——

Alan Granted!

Ian —but it might have been suicide, and with that hanging over
the place we couldn't start our life together here. There would
be such an unhappy atmosphere.

Jill Even though I love this flat, I couldn't be happy here if you
weren't. Let's go, darling.

Jill and Ian stand with their arms round each other

Ian (*suddenly*) Damn Charlie Baxter! I wish he hadn't told me.
I never did like him very much.

Alan (*enthusiastically*) You know, I rather like him after all. He
has hidden depths. A man after my own heart. Now they *must*
stay. Do something, darling. You must!

Brenda I can't! You know we're new to all this.

Ian and Jill move towards the door. Jill stops and gazes around

Jill How disappointing! It's such a lovely flat, and somehow I
really feel a happy one.

Brenda It was! It is! We were madly happy here, and so in love.
Please, please stay.

Ian Sorry, my love! I'm superstitious, I really am. Suicide!
Ugh! (*He shudders*)

Jill Come on! After all, there's lots of other flats.

Brenda But not like this one. It's you, it's really *you*, this one.

Ian and Jill turn to the door. Just as they do so, Miss Watson's head comes round it. She is about eighty, very brusque in her speech, and very severe-looking

Alan That's all we needed. Old Mother Watson. Now we are sunk.
Ian (*surprised*) Oh, hallo!
Miss Watson Saw the light on. Wondered who was here.
Alan Nosey old bag!

Miss Watson enters. She walks with a stick

Miss Watson Been looking over the flat?
Ian Er—yes!
Miss Watson Like it?
Jill I love it.
Alan She did, but you'll definitely put her off.
Miss Watson So you're taking it.
Jill Well—er, no! I'm afraid we're not.
Miss Watson Why not?
Ian Well, we've—we've decided against it.
Miss Watson Decided against it? (*To Jill*) But you said you loved it. (*She moves to the window, walking with slight difficulty with her stick*)
Brenda She's mad about it. They both are. Do something, Pegs!
Alan (*dumbfounded*) Pegs! Are you calling her "Pegs"? *Her?*
Brenda Her real name is Margaret.
Miss Watson (*at the window*) Lovely view from here.

Ian and Jill stand looking at Miss Watson rather helplessly

Jill Yes, it is.
Miss Watson Of course, you can't see much now.
Ian No, it's too dark.
Alan Now I call that really observant.
Miss Watson It's beautiful in the summer, y'know.
Alan Margaret, Pegs! How the blazes do you work that out?
Jill I'm sure it is.
Brenda Peggy is an abbreviation of Margaret, you ass!
Alan You could have fooled me. But *her*—Pegs!
Miss Watson But in the spring it's gorgeous.

Jill Oh yes, I'm sure it must be.

Alan But how did you know her name was Margaret, let alone Pegs?

Brenda Sh! Sh!

Alan What are you shushing for? They can't hear us.

Miss Watson The gardens are a perfect picture then.
    "When Spring comes back with rustling shade
    And apple-blossoms fill the air . . ."

Alan Good God! She's quoting poetry!

Brenda Why not? She's very well read.

Alan (*baffled*) But how do you *know* all this?

Miss Watson (*turning*) So why have you decided against it?

Ian Oh—er, just reasons.

Miss Watson Rent? Sorry, rude of me. Must forgive an old woman.

Ian Oh yes, certainly.

Brenda (*going to Miss Watson*) Pegs darling, do something— please!

Alan What's all this "Pegs darling"? I didn't know you knew her. I thought you didn't like her.

Brenda I did. You didn't.

Miss Watson Is it the rent?

Jill Well, no, not exactly.

Miss Watson What then?

Alan You've got to admire the old battle-axe. She comes straight to the point.

Jill Well, to be perfectly frank, my fiancé—that is to say, we don't think we'd be happy here.

Miss Watson Why not?

Alan You, for a start. (*To Ian*) Go on, chum, tell her to take a running jump.

Miss Watson You're both in love, aren't you?

Jill Yes, of course we are.

Miss Watson Then with that you'd be happy anywhere.

Alan With you a hundred miles away, possibly.

Miss Watson (*to Ian*) Your fiancée loves the flat.

Jill Yes, I do!

Miss Watson And it's not the rent.

Ian Well, no!

Miss Watson Then it's you! Why?

Alan Tell her the bedroom's too small. Go on, I dare you!

Ian Well, for one thing the bedroom is rather on the small side.

Alan (*highly delighted*) He heard me. He must have done. (*Shouting*) Now tell her to buzz off and mind her own business.

Miss Watson Fiddlesticks!

Ian Eh?

Miss Watson I said fiddlesticks! (*To Jill*) Do you think the bedroom is too small?

Jill No!

Miss Watson Well then, why?

Ian (*helplessly looking at Jill, who refuses to meet his glance*) Well —well—for—er—various reasons.

Miss Watson Name one.

Alan She sounds like a proper old school marm.

Brenda She was. She was a headmistress.

Alan Was she! Speak up, chum, otherwise you're in for six of the best.

Jill It's silly, I know—I mean *we* know, but . . .

Miss Watson It's not you. It's—him!

Jill (*determinedly*) Yes, it is!

Miss Watson That's obvious.

She moves over to Ian, who retreats slightly

Well, young man, do you love this young lady?

Ian (*indignantly*) Of course I do.

Miss Watson Do you want to make her happy?

Ian More than anything else in the world.

Alan He does improve on acquaintance. Even the old gorgon does! (*To Miss Watson*) Go on! You've got him reeling. Now knock him for six!

Miss Watson Then take this flat and make her happy and don't listen to stupid stories.

Ian Stupid stories?

Miss Watson That's what I said. Met old man Withers downstairs. Nice man, but a bit of an old woman.

Alan Coming from her that's hardly a compliment.

Miss Watson I don't know you, young man, but I think you're a bit of a fool. I hope you stay here and make me change my opinion.

Ian What do you mean?

Miss Watson turns from Ian, moves back to the window and stands gazing out. They all look at her

Miss Watson (*suddenly*) I knew the Ashwells.
Jill You knew them?
Miss Watson Yes. Well, at least, her more than him.
Alan (*to Brenda*) Did she? You never told me.
Miss Watson I miss them.
Alan Miss us! You miss us?
Miss Watson They were young, full of life, and very, very much in love.

Alan and Brenda move close to each other

    I used to come in here often to have tea or morning coffee with her. She was very sweet and understanding to an old woman.
Alan (*to Brenda*) I never knew this. I thought . . .
Brenda Why should you? You never liked her.
Miss Watson (*surprisingly giving vent to a chuckle*) For some unknown reason I put the fear of God into him. Used to amuse me. So like my nephew. I'm very fond of my nephew. Fond of Ashwell too, because he idolized his wife. I liked that. Yes, I miss them.
Ian But they committed suicide.
Miss Watson Fiddlesticks! Believe that and you'll believe anything. Suicides always leave a note to justify their action. They didn't. Accidental death was the verdict. They came back from a party that night. They were—well . . .
Ian Sloshed?
Alan And how!
Miss Watson Not a word I'd use myself but they were exceedingly merry. Living in the next flat, I heard them come in. He came out of the lift singing, for some extraordinary reason, the "Eton Boating Song"! I don't think he went to Eton.
Alan I don't remember that.
Brenda You did! You were making a shocking noise.
Miss Watson I'm afraid that she, too, was rather—er . . .
Ian Intoxicated?

Miss Watson Thank you. She tried to silence him as she herself endeavoured to render the Harrow School song "Forty Years On"!

Alan And you certainly didn't go to Harrow.

Miss Watson I thought at the time what an odd choice on both their parts. But they were obviously in a very happy mood.

Ian They must have been to quite a party.

Alan And how!

Miss Watson They evidently went into the bedroom and at some time turned on the gas fire.

Ian So?

Miss Watson They forgot to put a match to it—quite easily done in their bemused condition.

Jill Oh no!

Miss Watson At least they never knew. They just went off to sleep.

Alan (*holding Brenda close*) Oh, darling, darling, forgive me. I didn't know what I was doing.

Brenda Don't, darling, don't. It's over now, and we're still together.

Alan (*to Brenda*) I always said we should have had central heating.

Miss Watson I do miss them, and they'll never know how much.

Alan (*quietly*) We do, you old battle-axe. We do. (*He moves to Miss Watson and kisses her cheek*) I wish I had known you better, bless you!

Miss Watson (*pulling herself together*) Well, that's the true story. Take the advice of an old woman and have the flat. (*She moves to the door and stands there*) Y'know, I feel they left a lot of love behind. Why don't you share it? (*She looks at Jill and Ian and suddenly smiles*) I won't say good-bye—I somehow feel that *au revoir* will be more appropriate.

Miss Watson exits

Brenda Darling Pegs, you've done it.

Jill (*going to Ian*) Don't you feel it, all around you, darling? She's right, you know, she really is.

Ian (*suddenly holding her close and kissing her*) You know, darling, I don't really mind the tiny bedroom. Let's get down to old Withers and clinch it. (*He pulls her to the door and looks around the room*) *Au revoir!*

Ian switches out the light and they both exit, closing the door.
     The stage is left in darkness except for a very faint light from the window. A moment later we hear Jill's voice

Jill (*off*) Just a moment, darling, I forgot my umbrella.

The door opens again and Jill enters, switching on the light. The room is empty. She goes back to the window, picks up the umbrella, then moves back to the door. Then she stops and gazes round the room

(*Softly and happily*) We're going to be so happy.
Brenda (*her voice seemingly a long, long way away*) You will. You will.
Alan (*his voice a long way off, too*) We'll see to that.

Jill suddenly quickly turns, her head poised as though she had heard something. Then she shakes her head. No, it was just her imagination. She switches out the light, exits and closes the door, as—

the CURTAIN *slowly falls*

FURNITURE AND PROPERTY LIST

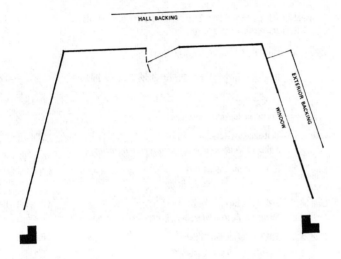

HALL BACKING

EXTERIOR BACKING

WINDOW

No furniture on stage

Personal: **Jill:** umbrella

LIGHTING PLOT

Property fittings required: 1 plain electric bulb pendant
  Interior. An empty room

To open: Effect of late afternoon light

Room almost dark. Faint glow from window

Cue 1	Voices heard in hall *Snap on light in hall*	(Page 2)
Cue 2	**Withers** switches on light *Snap on bulb and general interior lighting*	(Page 3)
Cue 3	**Ian** switches off light *Return to opening lighting*	(Page 18)
Cue 4	**Jill** switches on light *Snap on bulb and general interior lighting*	(Page 18)
Cue 5	**Jill** switches off light *Return to opening lighting*	(Page 18)